MY STORY, MY GIFT

HOW I BECAME AN EGG DONOR

DONOR CONCEPTION NETWORK

Text by Nina Barnsley and Stephanie Clarkson
Illustrations by Gabi Froden
Editing and Project Management by Stephanie Clarkson
Designed by Andy Archer
Produced by the 38a The Shop www.38atheshop.com
Published by the Donor Conception Network

Acknowledgements

The Donor Conception Network would like to thank the April Trust for their support in the production of these new **Our Story** books.

ISBN: 978-1-910222-85-0

Our Story 029 EGGDONOR/KNOWNFAMILY

This is a story about
something I did.

Something I feel
very proud of.

I want to share it with you so you
know about it, too.

I was so happy when you
arrived in our family.

I feel incredibly lucky that I was
able to have children.

Not everyone is as lucky as me.

It can be really hard to want a family
and for that not to happen.

There are lots of people who can't
have children without help.

To make a baby you need sperm
from a man, an egg from a woman and
a warm tummy to grow the baby in.

In most families the sperm comes
from the dad, the egg comes from
the mum and the baby grows in
her tummy, but...

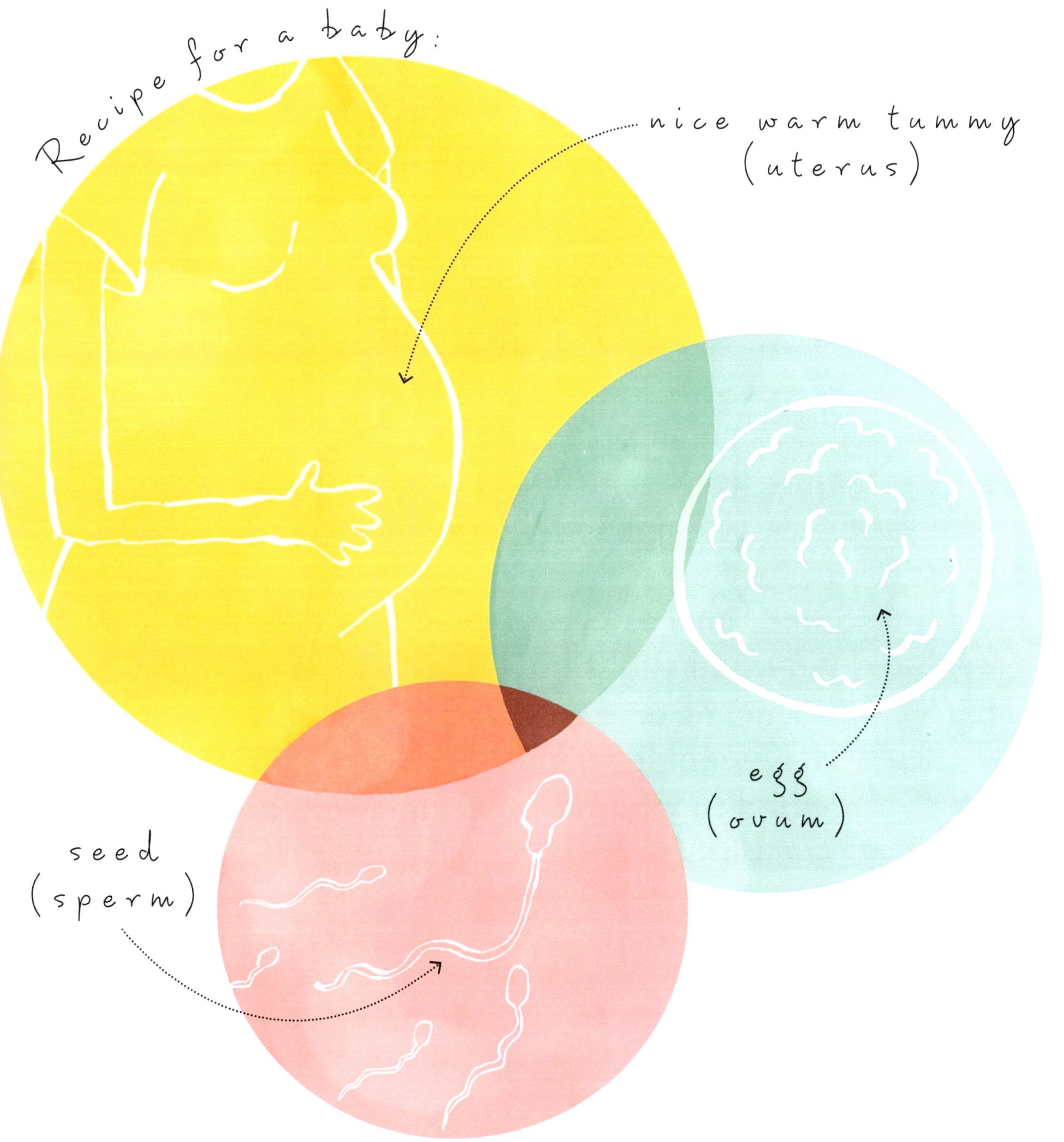

Recipe for a baby:
nice warm tummy (uterus)
egg (ovum)
seed (sperm)

...of course, it doesn't always
happen like that.

Sometimes the sperm or eggs or
tummy don't work properly or aren't able
to make or grow a baby.

Some families are formed in a different
way and might have two dads or two
mums or a single mum or dad.
They wouldn't have all the ingredients
needed to make a baby and would need
a bit of extra help, like sperm or
eggs from someone else.

CLINIC

Luckily, there are people who are happy
to give some of their sperm or eggs to help.
They are called donors.

Women sometimes offer to grow a baby
in their tummy for another family.
These women are called surrogates.

People become donors or surrogates to
help others who want to have children.

I thought about what it would be like
not to have children if you wanted them.

I wondered what I could do to help.

I realised I could become a
donor and give some of my eggs to
help someone who needed them.

So I went to a clinic and
that's what I did!

CLINIC

There are many different ways
that families are made and they
come in all shapes and sizes.

I know the people I helped.
I can tell you a bit about
them if you like.

I love our family and can't imagine
not having you in my life.

I feel very proud that I became an egg
donor and gave people a chance to have
the family they always dreamed of.